D0531964

Style Secrets

JEWELRY

TIPS & TRICKS

EMMA CARLSON BERNE

ILLUSTRATED BY ELENA HESCHKE

Lerner Publications ◆ Minneapolis

Lerner Publications Company
A division of Lerner Publishing Group, Inc.
241 First Avenue North
Minneapolis, MN 55401 USA

For reading levels and more information, look up this title at www.lernerbooks.com.

Main body text set in Grotesque MT Std. Light 10/14.
Typeface provided by Monotype.

Library of Congress Cataloging-in-Publication Data

Berne, Emma Carlson, author.
    Jewelry tips & tricks / By Emma Carlson Berne ; illustrated by Elena Heschke.
        pages cm. — (Style secrets)
    Includes index.
    ISBN 978-1-4677-5220-6 (lib. bdg. : alk. paper)
    ISBN 978-1-4677-8654-6 (EB pdf)
    1. Jewelry making—Juvenile literature. 2. Handicraft—Juvenile literature.
  I. Heschke, Elena, illustrator. II. Title. III. Title: Jewelry tips and tricks.
  TT212.B497 2016
  745.594'2—dc23   2014021869

Manufactured in the United States of America
1 – VP – 7/15/15

CONTENTS

Introduction

THE JEWELRY FACTOR

Since the beginning of our history, humans have decorated their hair, clothing, and bodies. Jewelry is a great way to say, "This is me, world!" Earrings, necklaces, bracelets, rings, pins, hair clips: all these can add sparkle and color to your outfit. You might put on a big, bright pair of earrings when you're out with friends or wear a small, delicate necklace to a concert or a play. Jewelry can also remind you of special times or people. Maybe your grandmother or your aunt has given you a bracelet you wear to remember her.

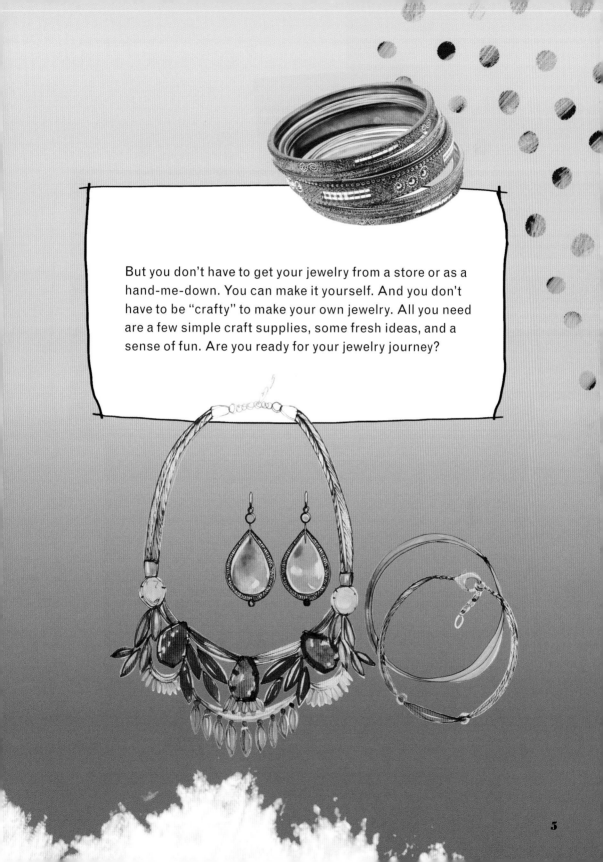

But you don't have to get your jewelry from a store or as a hand-me-down. You can make it yourself. And you don't have to be "crafty" to make your own jewelry. All you need are a few simple craft supplies, some fresh ideas, and a sense of fun. Are you ready for your jewelry journey?

Chapter 1

JEWELRY SUPPLIES

Becoming a master jewelry maker doesn't have to be expensive. But you will need to gather some basic supplies before you begin. You may find these items around your home. Also check grocery stores, drugstores, or craft stores. Thrift shops and garage sales can offer tons of interesting, inexpensive items. And ask neighbors or relatives if they have old odds and ends they'd like to get rid of.

Start by collecting small decorative items that either can be glued or have holes in them for stringing. Beads, buttons, crystals, feathers, and fake jewels are classic go-to items. And stock up on some less obvious options too. What about dried seeds, beans, or silk flowers? Even metal nuts and washers from the hardware store can fit the bill. Ditto for zippers, tassels, paper clips, and rubber bands. And keep an eye out for old decorative pins or brooches with fairly flat surfaces. You can take these apart and transform them into new jewelry. Some jump rings and clasps from a craft store—or from old jewelry—could come in handy too.

For stringing, gather yarn, elastic, string, or heavy thread. (Check out page 13 for more details on those.) You'll also need some fabric. Old clothes work great. That awesome shirt that's getting too holey to wear? That dress with the small unbeatable stain? Cut around the damaged parts and use the rest. Check your closet and nearby thrift stores for material you can upcycle. If you have any money to spare, scout a fabric store or order some fabrics online.

Stay Organized!

As you're building your supply of jewelry materials, make sure you're always able to find what you need. Rinse out some empty metal food cans or plastic cups. Then fill them with your beads, buttons, and other small items. You might keep all your beads in one container, or you might have so many beads that you separate them by color, shape, or size. If you're worried about spills, use containers with lids—like old metal breath mint boxes, spice containers, or jam jars. Keep one container for random items that don't belong with anything else in your collection.

YOUR JEWELRY TOOLBOX

Making jewelry is a little like cooking. You need your ingredients—what will go into each individual project—and your tools, which you'll reuse many times. Instead of bowls and measuring spoons, the basic tools for jewelry making include scissors, a small pair of pliers, tweezers, tape, and glue. Invest in these up front, and they'll serve you well for a long time.

<u>Glue.</u> Remember the school glue you used in art projects? It can work for making jewelry too. But you'll also want a stronger type of glue for objects that have trouble staying stuck. Check out the selection of craft glue at stores or online. Compare prices and read the labels. (Some glues give off harmful fumes or can damage skin. Nine times out of ten, you won't need anything that intense for your jewelry projects.)

<u>Measurement aids.</u> Making jewelry is all about having a good eye. But when it comes to deciding the length of a necklace string or the width of a bracelet, eyeballing isn't ideal. Instead, use a ruler or a tape measure. A tape measure is extra handy because it's flexible—perfect for loops and curves.

Pliers. Not all pliers are created equal. They come in different sizes and shapes, and they work in different ways. For jewelry making, it's helpful to have a pair of needle-nose pliers. These pliers are long with thin, sharp tips. They can be used for holding, bending, and cutting objects. They're especially handy for working with small, delicate items. If you don't have pliers, tweezers can be a good substitute, except when it comes to cutting.

Tape. Clear tape can wrap around the tip of a pin or an earring to keep it from poking you. And tape can temporarily hold pieces of your jewelry puzzle in place while you're assembling everything. Duct tape and electrical tape come in bright colors and fun patterns. So you might just want to add some to that finicky clasp or that scratched-up bracelet.

When you're working on jewelry, cover your work area with newspaper to catch glue drips. And work near an open window if you're using heavy-duty craft glue or other products that give off fumes. Make sure you have a damp rag to wipe your hands—plus plenty of time and patience.

SMART STORAGE

Before you start adding to your jewelry collection, create some storage space for your bling. You can buy jewelry boxes or hanging, pocketed jewelry organizers—or you can make your own. Use an empty metal breath-mint container for rings or earrings. Add cardboard dividers to a larger box to keep individual bracelets and necklaces separate. Or try hanging jewelry from pushpins on a corkboard. Use your imagination and common sense to rig up a system that works for you.

JEWELRY HANGER

With only some nails, a wooden clothes hanger, and a hammer, you can make a funky and simple jewelry organizing system.

What You Need:

- 10 to 20 small nails
- an old wooden clothes hanger
- a thick wooden board larger than the hanger
- a stable work surface, such as a table or the floor
- a hammer
- craft supplies of your choice (school glue, scissors, markers, paint, glitter, or whatever you like)

Here's How:

1. Get an adult's permission to bang nails into the hanger.

2. Place the wooden board on your work surface. Lay the hanger and nails out on top of the board.

3. Carefully hammer the nails into the wide side of the hanger, evenly spaced. Don't nail them all the way in—leave them sticking out by ¼ to 1½ inches (0.6 to 3.8 centimeters). (If you accidentally hammer a nail too far in, don't worry. The wooden board under the hanger will protect your larger work surface. Use the claw of the hammer to pull the nail back out.)

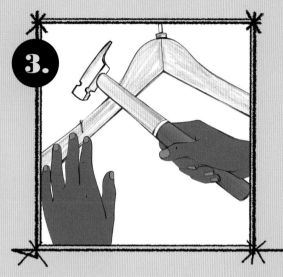

4. Decorate the hanger. You might choose to paint the letters of your name between the nails. Or you might cover the hanger with glue and sprinkle a layer of glitter all over it. It's up to you! If you use glue, wait about 15 minutes for it to dry.

5. Hang the hanger on a hook, a door handle, or a closet rack.

6. Place your necklaces, bracelets, rings, and earrings over the nails.

Chapter 2

NICE NECKLACE!

Jewelry doesn't get much simpler than a necklace. If you've got something you can tie around your neck—a piece of string, a ribbon, a chain—you're set. But from there, a necklace could turn into almost anything you can imagine. It might be a valuable string of pearls from your grandmother. Or it can be as inexpensive as a cool key you found and strung on a piece of yarn. You could wear a string of beads reaching to your waist. Or you could go for a single delicate charm on a small chain.

Lots of materials can turn into necklaces. So which ones should you make sure to keep on hand? It's up to you, but here are some options. Stock up on those you'll likely use most. You can get smaller amounts of other materials as you need them. And don't worry if you can't afford the fancy stuff. The most basic materials often work just as well as pricier specialty supplies. If it's easy to work with and strong enough to last awhile, it'll make great jewelry.

<u>Cords and ropes.</u> Nylon, cotton, faux leather, imitation suede, and more: you can use all types of cords to string a necklace. Utility rope from a hardware store is strong but flexible. Thick, braided cord isn't ideal for stringing decorative elements, but it comes in vibrant colors, and you can knot it to make a unique pattern.

<u>Fabrics.</u> Whether it's cotton, velvet, silk, or jersey, fabric can make a solid foundation for a necklace. Ribbons and cloth strips often work best as chokers, rather than loose-hanging loops.

<u>Chains and wires.</u> Metal isn't the coziest necklace material, but it can be perfect for stringing beads or buttons. It's also hard to tie a knot in a chain or a wire, so you may need to pick up some jump rings and clasps to complete your necklace. You can find these at craft stores and hardware stores.

<u>Strings and threads.</u> Many craft and jewelry stores sell thin beading thread. Use elastic if you like the stretchy factor. Pricier, stronger specialty threads hold their shape best. But plain string, yarn, or sewing thread can work too.

Before you begin making a necklace, measure the length of string or fabric you're using. In front of a mirror, hold a long length of string around your neck. Mark the length you want. Add an extra 6 inches (15 cm). That will leave you plenty of room for tying the ends together. If you have trouble deciding how long you want your necklace to be, unlatch and lay out another necklace you already have. Add 6 inches to that length and cut the string. Then you're ready to go!

NECKLACES UNLIMITED

So you have all your materials ready. What kind of necklace are you going to make? The good news is you don't have to choose just one. Try as many different styles as you want!

Chokers. A choker fits snugly around the neck. You can make a comfortable one out of a ribbon or a thicker strip of fabric. To decorate a choker, use craft glue to attach sequins, small beads, or even colored thread.

Pendants. These simple necklaces add a dash of elegance or flair. If you've got a cord, a string, or a chain, the work of making a pendant is half done. Just hang an eye-catching item, such as an old earring, from the string in the middle. If you want, string a few smaller objects on either side.

Rope necklaces. You can find synthetic cords in a wide range of colors and patterns at dollar stores, hardware stores, and craft stores. If one loop isn't exciting enough for you, wind a longer cord around your neck several times. Or combine cords of different colors or designs for a layered look. Spice up a thin cord necklace by stringing decorative items on it.

BUTTON NECKLACE

A button necklace is a simple and colorful piece that you can wear to school, out with friends, or for a dress-up event.

What You Need:
- a flexible tape measure
- scissors
- cotton string or yarn
- tape
- 25 to 75 buttons in the size(s) you want

Here's How:

1. Measure and cut the string to your preferred necklace length (plus 6 inches, or 15 cm).

2. Tie a knot a few inches from one end of the string.

3. Tape the knot end of the string to a table or other surface.

4. String your buttons. Pass one eye of each button through the string so that the button's edge will face out when you wear the necklace. (For some variety, try passing both eyes of a button through the string. That way, the flat side of the button will face out.)

5. Tie a knot in the other end of the string. Be sure not to make the button string too tight—the buttons need to have some room to move on the string, so they don't pinch your neck.

6. Facing a mirror, hold the necklace up to your neck and adjust the length by tightening or loosening the string.

7. Tie the ends at the length you want. If your necklace is too small to get the necklace over your head, tie the ends in a bow so you can easily tie and untie them. Go show off your new necklace!

Button Blueprint

When you choose your buttons for this necklace, think about the overall visual effect you want to create. Decide on a blueprint for your necklace—a color scheme and a pattern—before you start stringing. Do you want to use buttons that are different shades of one main color? Do you want to alternate small and large buttons? Or would you prefer contrasting colors and sizes?

FABRIC AND COTTON BALL NECKLACE

When you're looking for jewelry with a soft touch that still makes a big impression, a fabric necklace fits the bill. Fabric is more comfortable and more flexible than most jewelry materials. But it doesn't have to just blend in with your clothing. This fabric necklace is large and bold. It flatters a simple top. You won't need any other jewelry when you wear this hard-to-miss piece.

What You Need:

* a tape measure (optional)
* a hollow tube of fabric at least 2 feet (0.6 meters) long, such as a bathrobe belt
* 20 cotton balls (or 5 to 8 other round, light objects, such as large acorns or large beads)
* scissors

Here's How:

1. Measure a length of fabric twice as long as the necklace you want to make. You'll need plenty of extra fabric for inserting the cotton balls and tying knots.

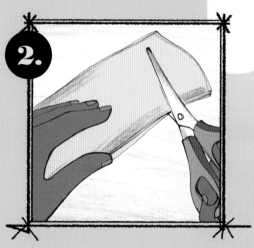

2. Open the tube of fabric by cutting open one end, and fold back the open end.

3. Tie a knot in the closed end of the fabric tube, about 5 inches (13 cm) from the end.

4. Poke three cotton balls (or one acorn or bead) into the tube, working them down until they are snug against the knot.

5. Tie another knot on the other side of the object, holding it in place between the two knots.

6. Repeat steps 3, 4, and 5 until your necklace is the length you want.

7. Leave about 5 inches at the open end so you can tie off your necklace.

8. Tie the ends of the necklace in a knot and try it on. How does it look?

Mix It Up!

If you want to make a different kind of fabric necklace, try inserting larger objects, such as Ping-Pong balls. Try alternating small beads with large ones as you tie knots. Try another fabric, such as see-through chiffon. What does that look like when you insert large colored beads?

Chapter 3
BRING ON THE BRACELETS

Woven, strung, bangles, cuffs . . . bracelets come in countless different types. They draw attention to your hands and arms. They can be very casual, such as a denim cuff. Or they can be super elegant and made of pearls or jewels.

If you have some string and a handful of small, interesting objects with holes in them, then you can make your own bracelet. For instance, stringing cool old keys makes a jangly, funky bracelet. Ever seen old wooden buttons on an overcoat? How about putting some of those buttons on a leather cord around your wrist? A seashell might have a natural hole at one end—a perfect, delicate bracelet material. You could string those on silk cord for a softer look.

Making your own bracelets isn't difficult. You can use the same materials you've gathered for necklace making. But one very important factor sets bracelets apart: you must make sure they are the right length. Unlike necklaces, which can be a wide variety of sizes, bracelets have to be just wide enough to fit over your hand, but not so wide that they will fall off your wrist. Carefully measure your material to the length you like before you start getting creative.

ALL KINDS OF BRACELETS

You can make—or make over—any type of bracelet. No matter what you do, don't be afraid to make mistakes. Experimenting, messing up, and trying again are all marks of a great artist and craftsperson.

<u>Bangles.</u> A true bangle holds its shape no matter what. Bangles are often made of wood, metal, or plastic. Turn a plain bangle into jaw-dropping wrist wear by adding sequins, glitter, or painted designs.

<u>Charms.</u> If your bracelet has anything dangling off it—feathers, metal pieces, hanging beads—it counts as a charm bracelet. Use jump rings to attach new trinkets to a plain chain bracelet.

<u>Cuffs.</u> These open-ended bracelets are easy to slide onto your wrist and then clamp for a tight fit. They're usually made of fairly stiff material, especially metals and plastics. Read on to find out how to make your own!

DIY Tape Measure

If you don't have a flexible tape measure, don't worry. Just cut a strip of paper and wrap it around your wrist. Mark the place where the paper overlaps. Then stretch the paper out on a ruler and start measuring.

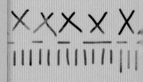

SAFETY PIN BRACELET

For a fun, relaxed look, try this easy-to-make bracelet.

What You Need:

- a flexible tape measure
- 2 stiff pieces of string (twine, leather thong, or elastic cord), measured to the length you want
- at least 50 safety pins
- scissors
- tape

Here's How:

1. Wrap the tape measure around your wrist so that it is snug but not tight. Note the length. Then add 4 inches (10 cm). That will leave you enough string to tie the ends.

2. Line up the two strings and tie them together about 3 inches (7.5 cm) from the top.

3. Tape the knotted end to a table.

4. Thread one string through the hole at the top of a safety pin (where the clasp encloses the sharp pin part) and the other string through the coil at the bottom of the safety pin.

5. Slide the pin down both strings until it is flush against the knot.

6. Repeat this, alternating the safety pins top to bottom. If you slid the string through the top on one pin, for the next one, slide that string through the bottom. Since safety pins are fatter at the top than at the bottom, this will keep your bracelet even. Remember not to slide the safety pins too close together. They need to be able to shift on the string loosely so the bracelet can wrap around your wrist.

7. When you're done stringing the safety pins, tie the two strings together at the other end. This will keep your pins from falling off.

8. Try on your bracelet and mark the spot for the final knot.

9. Tie the two ends together in the length you want. Remember to keep the bracelet a little loose—you have to be able to slide it over your hand.

10. Try your bracelet on and spread out the safety pins.

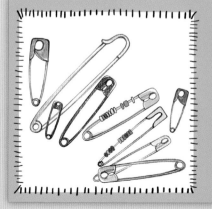

Put a New Spin on It

Once you've mastered this basic design, you can experiment with different kinds of safety pin bracelets. Use gold pins, very large pins, tiny pins—or even old-fashioned diaper pins, if you can find them! Or thread tiny colored beads onto your safety pins before pinning them closed and stringing them.

FABRIC CUFF BRACELET

This bracelet is perfect for school or for going out with friends. It takes about half an hour to make.

What You Need:

- newspaper
- a flexible tape measure
- scissors
- a piece of lace, chiffon, or other filmy material
- plastic wrap
- a damp sponge
- a bowl of water
- washable school glue
- tape
- a blow-dryer (optional)
- a damp rag for wiping fingers

Here's How:

1. Spread out the newspaper to protect your surface. Place your supplies on it.

2. Use the tape measure to measure your wrist. Cut a piece of fabric the length of your wrist minus 1 inch (2.5 cm) and 3 to 4 inches (7.6 to 10 cm) wide.

3. Cover your wrist, but not your hand, with plastic wrap and secure with a piece of tape.

4. Dampen the sponge in the water. Set it aside for the moment.

5. Squeeze glue all over one side of the fabric.

6. Working quickly, use the sponge to smear the glue evenly and thickly over the fabric. Make sure the cloth is completely covered. (This will be messy.)

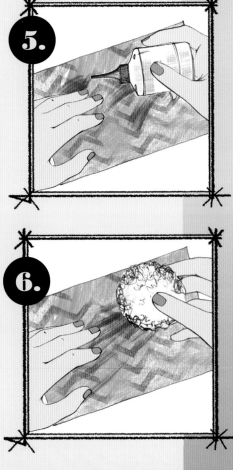

7. Flip the cloth and spread glue on the other side, smearing thickly and evenly with the sponge.

8. Drape the wet, gluey fabric over your plastic-wrap-covered wrist.

9. Wait about 15 minutes for the glue to dry and the cuff to harden. You can help the glue dry faster by blasting it with a blow-dryer. (Don't burn your wrist!)

10. Touch the fabric gently to check the dryness.

11. When the glue is *completely* dry, slide a finger under the fabric and pull it slowly off the plastic wrap. Try to lift it, rather than peel. This will help keep the curved shape.

12. Take the plastic wrap off your wrist and throw it away.

13. Put the cuff on and squeeze it around your wrist to help it regain its shape. Nice work!

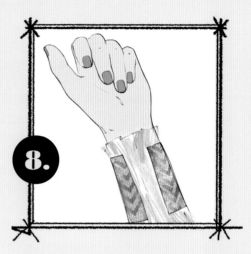

<u>Fabulous Fabrics</u>

Experiment with a different material for your next fabric cuff. How does it look in chiffon? What about T-shirt material, such as jersey? You don't even have to limit yourself to fabrics. You might try cutting a slit in a paper towel roll, for instance. Trim the roll down to cuff size and cover it with duct tape in wild colors.

Chapter 4

BRILLIANT BLING

Ornaments are among the most flexible pieces of jewelry. These small accent pieces add touches of class or bursts of pizazz to your look. A ring can bring sparkle to any finger (or to a toe). Earrings—from studs to hoops to danglers—are easy to customize, whether you have pierced ears or not.

And let's not forget pins. Fashion pins come in all shapes and sizes, and you can stick them on almost any item of clothing. A pin can decorate a jacket or a sweater. Or it can clip onto a hat or a belt. Use a hairpin to hold back a strand of hair, or tuck that pin into a braid or a bun for an extra pop.

It's a snap to make your own ornaments. Visit a thrift store, or collect old ornaments from relatives or neighbors. To make a decorative pin, all you need is an old pin with a fairly flat surface to use as a base. The same goes for rings—you can transform the original band into something totally new. Or you can make a ring from scratch using wire, elastic, or thread.

As for earrings, you can find posts and earring backs—or clips for unpierced ears—at craft stores or online. Attach these to dangly fragments of old necklaces or bracelets, strings of beads, or even old zipper pulls. You can also redecorate old earrings so that they're unrecognizable!

COMBINATION EARRINGS

Don't have pierced ears? Don't worry! It's easy to turn pierced earrings into clips. It's equally easy—and even more fun—to combine a pair of clip-ons with a pair of pierced earrings.

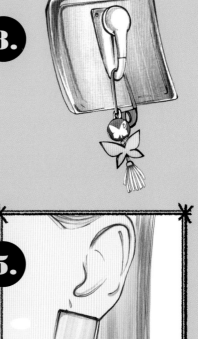

What You Need:

- a pair of small clip-on earrings with a plain front
- two very small safety pins
- pierced earrings with posts or closed loops (don't use earrings with hooks; large, dangling earrings work best)

Here's How:

1. If you're using closed loop earrings, slide the loop over the clip at the back of the clip-on earring. That's all it takes!

2. If you're using post earrings, slide the safety pin over the clip at the back of the clip-on earring.

3. Insert the post into the small hole at the top or bottom of the safety pin.

4. Replace the post backing.

5. Clip on your earring combo and enjoy!

TO PIERCE OR NOT TO PIERCE?

Should you get your ears pierced? If you're weighing that question, consider the pros and cons. On the con side, a piercing costs money and it does hurt, if only for a second. On the pro side, pierced earrings are easier to keep in your ears. And they come in more styles than clip-ons. You can do a lot with clips, but not all regular earrings can be converted to or combined with clip-ons. (Think stud earrings.) So if you're a big earring fan, you'll have more options with pierced ears.

If you decide to pierce your ears, never allow a friend to do it or try it at home yourself. You should only go to a reputable jewelry or piercing shop, where a trained piercer can put in your new earrings. And make sure you get a parental thumbs-up first. You'll need to bring an adult along when you go for your piercing.

Once you've made the leap, take good care of your holes while they're healing. Only wear the studs you are given by the person who pierced your ears. Follow your piercer's care instructions closely, and call the shop if you have questions. Otherwise, you can wind up with infected holes and even scars.

FANCY FEATHER EARRINGS

Use feathers to dress up an old, boring pair of earrings! You can find craft feathers in many colors—or you can get plain white ones and jazz them up with markers or acrylic paint.

What You Need:

- a pair of clip-on or pierced earrings
- pliers
- scissors
- assorted craft feathers, small to medium size
- craft glue

Here's How:

1. If your earrings already have plain, flat surfaces, you're ready to start. If your earrings have any decorations or dangling parts you don't want, use the pliers to pry or snip them off.

2. If you need to, snip the feathers so they are short enough or trim the edges if they are too wide.

3. Glue feathers to each earring in the pattern you want.

4. Let the earrings dry completely. Then enjoy wearing them!

Fabulous Feathers

You can use feathers in other ways too. Glue them to a headband or a decorative pin. Tuck one into your ponytail, flowing down, or weave a long, thin feather into a braid.

BLING FOR ALL OCCASIONS

You probably wouldn't wear your bathrobe to school, right? Or your coolest top to bed? Not all ornaments work for all situations either. At school, babysitting, or at an after-school job, it's usually best to wear small pieces that aren't distracting and won't get in your way. For instance, you might wear a sturdy hairpin or small stud earrings. You also probably don't want to go overboard at a formal event. For fancy occasions such as weddings or awards ceremonies, lean toward small-yet-sparkly pieces. But when you're hanging out with your friends or going to see a concert or a sports event, let yourself go! Load up your fingers with those neon rings, or proudly sport that wild pom-pom hairpin.

PERSONALIZED HAIRPIN

Maybe you have a decorative pin lying around that you'd like to spruce up. But you don't want to wear it on your clothes. What else can you do with it? Turn it into a hairpin! And make it stand out with decorative elements of your choice.

What You Need:

- pliers
- an old pin with a flat surface
- craft glue
- light beads, small buttons, or crystals
- a large bobby pin or barrette

1.

Here's How:

1. With the pliers, clip the clasp off the back of the pin.

2. Glue your bling in the pattern you want on the surface of the pin.

3. Wait about 15 minutes for the glue to dry completely.

4. Turn the pin over.

5. Run a thick line of glue along the back of the bobby pin or the barrette. Then press it gently onto the back of the pin.

6. Let it dry and try it on. Now you're ready for any occasion!

The Real Secret

Making your own jewelry is an adventure, whether you're starting from scratch or reusing old pieces in different ways. Try to think about your materials in new ways, not just in terms of what they are but in terms of what they *can* be.

String an old pin on a leather thong or a heavy cord. *Voilà!* You have a pendant. Cut apart old necklaces and restring them. You can combine parts of two old necklaces into one. You can even make a necklace into a bracelet by looping it a few times around your wrist. How about wearing an old ring on a string around your neck? Or poking a decorative pin into a hair bun as an ornament? (Just wrap a little tape around the pin tip so you don't poke yourself in the scalp!)

Jewelry is a form of art. You are the artist, and good artists try to see ordinary objects in different ways. You can be inspired by objects in your world to create unique jewelry for every occasion!

GLOSSARY

bangle: a stiff bracelet with no flexibility

blueprint: a plan

chiffon: a very thin, sheer fabric, often made of silk

choker: a necklace that fits closely around the neck

clasp: a fastening device that holds a necklace or a bracelet closed

jersey: a soft, knitted fabric often used for clothing

jump ring: a metal ring used to make jewelry

nut: a small piece of metal with a hole in it, for screwing onto a bolt

ornament: a small decorative item

pendant: a piece of jewelry that hangs from a cord, string, or chain around the neck

pliers: a tool with pincers for gripping and bending

thong: a narrow strip of leather, used for fastening

upcycle: to turn an item that would otherwise be thrown away into a new product

washer: a small, flat piece of metal with a hole in it

FURTHER INFORMATION

DIY Jewelry: Craft Foxes
http://www.craftfoxes.com/blog/tag/diy-jewelry
From duct tape bracelets to bling made from candy wrappers, this site collects fun and funky jewelry-making tutorials. You can also find lots of other crafts to test your creativity!

Dorsey, Colleen. *Totally Awesome Rubber Band Jewelry.* East Petersburg, PA: Design Originals, 2013. Make all kinds of bling from rubber bands.

Drew, Sarah. *Junk-Box Jewelry: 25 DIY Low Cost (or No Cost) Jewelry Projects.* San Francisco: Zest Books, 2012.

Jacobson, Ryan. *Get a Job Making Stuff to Sell.* Minneapolis: Lerner Publications, 2015. Find out how to make money selling homemade jewelry and other creations.

Nichols, Kaitlyn. *Toolbox Jewelry.* Palo Alto, CA: Klutz, 2013. Learn how to make jewelry from items you can find at the hardware store, and get started with the included materials!

Steele-Saccio, Eva. *Beaded Bands: Super Stylish Bracelets Made Simple.* Palo Alto, CA: Klutz, 2012. Easy bracelets look fancy when you're done, and this book comes with materials to get you started.

"Success Tips for a Teenage Jewelry Artist": *Jewelry Making Journal*
http://jewelrymakingjournal.com/jewelry-artist
Learn how to start and run your own jewelry business.

INDEX

PHOTO ACKNOWLEDGMENTS

The images in this book are used with the permission of: © HamsterMan/Shutterstock.com, pp. 1, 4 (bottom); © iStockphoto.com/transiastock, pp. 2, 6; © iStockphoto.com/deymos, p. 4 (top); © iStockphoto.com/Jasmin Awad, p. 5; © J. Palys/Shutterstock.com, p. 7; © PinkPueblo/iStock/Thinkstock, pp. 8-9; © RLN/Shutterstock.com, p. 9; © Planner/Shutterstock.com, p. 10 (bottom); © Cecillia Artclip/Shutterstock.com, p. 10 (top); © iStockphoto.com/vitapix, p. 12; © kritskaya/Shutterstock.com, p. 13; © Irina Mishina/Shutterstock.com, p. 14; © Magnia/Shutterstock.com, pp. 16-17; © daffodilred/Shutterstock.com, p. 18; © marine.t/Shutterstock.com, p. 20; © Art_girl/Shutterstock.com, pp. 24, 32; © MyImages - Micha/Shutterstock.com, p. 26 (top); © iStockphoto.com/Newbird, p. 26 (bottom); © severija/Shutterstock.com, pp. 28, 31; © Tatyanaego/Dreamstime.com, p. 29 (top); © iStockphoto.com/Elnur, p. 29 (bottom); © iStockphoto.com/transiastock, p. 30.

Front cover: © HamsterMan/Shutterstock.com.

Back cover: © severija/Shutterstock.com (glitter); © iStockphoto.com/Newbird (feathers); © HamsterMan/Shutterstock.com (jewels).